"IN GOD WE TRUST"?

"IN GOD WE TRUST"?

WHAT IS GOD SAYING IN THE MIDST OF THIS FINANCIAL CRISIS?

MICHAEL A. G. HAYKIN

Emmaus Road Publishing, Inc.
6705 Rustic Ridge Trail
Grand Blanc, Michigan 48439 USA
www.emmausroadpress.com

Audubon Press
& Christian Book Service
Audubon Press
2601 Audubon Drive, P.O. Box 8055
Laurel, Mississippi 39441-8000 USA
www.audubonpress.com

Unless otherwise indicated, all Scripture quotations are from The Holy Bible, English Standard Version. Copyright © 2001 by Crossway Bibles, a division of Good News Publishers. All rights reserved.

Cover design: Peter Cooper
Editorial design: Janice Van Eck

Library of Congress Cataloguing in Publication Data available

ISBN 978-0-9819831-0-3   PRINTED IN THE USA

FOREWORD

conomics is really a metaphysical science rather than a mathematical one in which the spiritual values and attitudes are more important than physical assets and the morality and virtue of the population as foundational as the money supply. Products and services are, in the end, the assembly of qualities and their value derives directly from the innate character and ideals of those who create them and the workmanship of those who produce them. Things are, in the final analysis, the representation of thoughts. Quality products come from quality thoughts, inferior products from inferior thoughts.

If this is true, an economy, like an individual business or a specific product or service, is the total of the spiritual and mental qualities of its people. The economic output of a country can never be stronger than the values of the society at large. Without the refining influence of strong moral standards, such as honesty, trust, integrity, loyalty and the golden rule, the marketplace quickly deteriorates. A society, particularly a free market society, that does not have strong ethical values cannot over the long term produce much of value; and a nation whose values are in decline will eventually witness a decline in its economy.

The financial crisis that now embroils the global economy should not have come as a surprise to Christians. The lack of ethics and standards throughout our culture has finally caught up with us financially. The baby boomers, those born between 1946 and 1964, who were born into so much privilege throughout many Western countries have, by and large, rejected the values of their parents and embraced an irresponsible and materialistic lifestyle, much of it purchased on a line of credit. Financial institutions willing to lend money in the short term detached themselves from ethical underwriting standards and provided capital to people who could never repay the loans. Often these same institutions, knowing they were creating substandard and inferior loans, sold them off to investors at inflated prices, thus setting up a chain of eventual losses that would run into trillions of U.S. dollars. Regulatory bodies set up for oversight purposes, in too many cases, knew what was happening but turned a blind eye and did nothing. In the drive for more things, more earnings and more votes, what people forgot was that an economy built on excessive debt simply cannot last!

The result was a dramatic lowering of almost all asset values globally and the freezing up of trust, otherwise known as credit, in the financial world. The losses now borne by investors and taxpayers are staggering. Now that the panic button has been pushed, it's time for Christians to take an honest look at the problem and bring biblical solutions to a world drowning in debt and unsustainable promises. All of us need to remember that growth in capital is a long-term process, underpinned by ethics, discipline, hard work and self-sacrifice.

Christians, in particular, should be part of the solution, since they can provide the necessary spiritual anchors in a postmodern culture plagued by short-term thinking. We need true leaders who will balance the needs of this generation with future generations and build a strong and responsible economy rooted in the enduring principles of biblical truth. Such leadership means nothing less than standing on biblical principles and never wavering from these principles. We need Christian leaders with deep character, vision, integrity, courage and understanding. If the Christian community will not step up to the leadership plate who will?

In practical terms this means we are to invest for the future as good stewards of the capital with which God has blessed us. We need to spend only what we have and avoid the awful trap of consumerism and materialism, even if this means less "things" in the days ahead. Michael Haykin's biblical response to the financial crisis gets to the heart of this issue as he looks at the biblical view of wealth and a number of historical examples of how Christians have used their wealth in powerful ways to further the kingdom of our Lord. In the midst of all the challenges, Christians can look to the future knowing that our God is sovereign and that, despite all the challenges we face, Jesus Christ has instructed us in his Word how we are to live and spend in this present age. And when all is said and done, we take strong comfort in the reality that Jesus Christ is on the throne and moving history forward to its appointed end.

JONATHAN WELLUM B.COMM., B.SC., MA, MBA, CFA
CEO & CIO, AIC Limited, Burlington, Ontario, Canada

No possessions are secure enough,
no wealth ample enough to give true happiness
without the favor of God. And with that,
one can have peace passing all understanding,
no matter what his earthly lot.
—*Basil Manly, Jr. (1825-1892)*

"IN GOD WE TRUST"?

WHAT IS GOD SAYING IN THE MIDST
OF THIS FINANCIAL CRISIS?[1]

The title of a recent book that deals with the current global financial crisis by former Wall Street insider Michael Lewis sums up the emotional response to this economic meltdown by many people in the West: *Panic*.[2] The current financial crunch has shaken and rattled the West to a depth that has not been seen since the 1930s, and not surprisingly some economic pundits are talking about a repeat of the Great Depression.[3] Now, it would be all too easy for a Christian looking at the financial mess of our Western societies—that began with the American subprime mortgage fiasco and has spread outwards, bringing ruination to the financial services sector and illiquidity to many businesses in the West—to say, "This is the end. God is judging the West for its sins."

About a decade ago, well-known preacher David Wilkerson did indeed write a book along these lines, *America's Last Call*, in which he predicted a "financial holocaust" and the "crippling of the American economy."[4] But this financial collapse is affecting far more than America. The entirety of Europe has been similarly impacted, with failing banks and the disappearance of financial liquidity.[5] Reverberations are also being felt in markets further afield. It is very true that there is a day coming when God will bring down to destruction the financial markets of the world and all who have trusted in those markets will be utterly devastated. Overwhelmed by the loss of all that they had trusted in, the Bible says that they will mourn and weep.[6] But there is no indication that this current crisis is that day,[7] which is one of the final events of history in God's judgment of the world.

Of course, there is real loss and pain that this current financial meltdown has brought about and that cannot be minimized. But if this is not the end of the world, what is God saying in the midst of it? It was the conviction of C. S. Lewis, the Oxford professor who is best known for his children's stories about Narnia, that "God whispers to us in our pleasures, speaks in our conscience, but shouts in our pains," for pain "is His megaphone to rouse a deaf world."[8] I am sure some might want to differ with certain aspects of this conviction, but Lewis is definitely right that when things go wrong, or break down, we begin to ask those profound questions that many of us tend to ignore in daily life. "Why did this happen?" we cry. "What does it all mean?" we query. Well, what *is* God saying in the midst of this financial mess?

LISTENING TO AUGUSTINE ABOUT TRUE WEALTH

In a recent book on financial history, the brilliant Scottish historian Niall Ferguson has observed that unlike other types of historians, who shy away from drawing distinct lessons from the past, those who study the history of economics do so in order to find ways to avoid repeating the economic disasters of the past.[9] I personally think that Ferguson's point can be applied to other fields of history as well. In other words, one of the reasons for reading about the past is to learn from the mistakes of those who have gone before us. While the past never repeats itself exactly,[10] there are enough general patterns in the past that we can study it and learn from prior error. As a famous proverb puts it: "He who does not remember the past is doomed to repeat it."[11]

In late August A.D. 410, Rome, the symbolic center of the once-mighty Roman Empire, was ransacked for three days by the barbarian Alaric and his horde of Visigothic warriors. Over the course of those three days, Rome went through what the North African theologian Augustine (A.D. 354-430), one of the great thinkers of early Christianity, would later describe as "devastation, butchery, [and] plundering."[12] A number of leading senators were slain, women were raped, even some who had devoted themselves to celibacy for Christ's sake, and other men and women were taken hostage.[13] Some lost everything they owned and escaped with nothing but the clothes on their backs.[14] To all of the questions raised by the enormity of this human suffering, Augustine sought at that time to give reasoned and biblical answers. What he said to those who lost their possessions during that time of devastation is, as we shall see, certainly applicable to those who have sustained losses, both great and small, in the current financial crunch.

Augustine began by insisting that while a Christian may lose all of his possessions, he can never lose the riches of faith and godliness. These things are lodged within a person, in his inner being, and can never be stolen or lost. Here Augustine quoted one of his mentors from the past, the Apostle Paul, who had written some 350 years earlier that "godliness with contentment is great gain."[15] A Christian's real wealth is his or her upright character, integrity and good deeds. If the Christian has such, along with "food and clothing," another citation from Paul,[16] and is moreover, content with this, then this is "great gain." In the final analysis, Augustine pointed out that all of the material possessions a person has in this world will cease to be his at death. And here he quoted from another biblical book, Job, in which the human subject of that book responds to the loss of his possessions like this: "Naked I came from my mother's womb, and naked shall I return. The Lord gave, and the Lord has taken away; blessed be the name of the Lord."[17] It is obvious that Augustine felt that this was the proper way to respond to the calamity of his day. Ultimately, a person is just a *steward* of everything he owns. His possessions are on loan to him, as it were, to be used properly, and then one day, when he leaves this world, they have to be relinquished. Augustine is clear that the problem does not lie in owning things, but in the unbounded desire for things, the immoderate hunger for more and more. Those people who are possessed by such a desire and hunger will find themselves trapped in "a snare" that will ultimately bring them to "ruin and destruction."[18]

An Augustinian response, then, to the present crisis, would be to remind those Christians who have lost significant wealth, and maybe even all of their savings, that this does not mean they have lost their true assets, namely, their faith, character and good works. Augustine would remind us that utter devastation of soul at such a time as this implies that we were finding our security and prosperity in *things*. And surely one of the besetting sins of our Western culture, and North America in particular, has been materialism and consumerism. Our culture has lost sight of the fact that a person's life does not consist in what he owns. The value of a person is not reducible to the size of his or her paycheck or bank account.

AUGUSTINE (354-430)

Portrait by Hélène Grondines © 2009

Sadly, in the recent past some Christians who have bought into this materialism. Some have lived their lives in ways that are appreciably little different from the ways of their non-Christian neighbors. They have indulged the same desires for status and privilege. They have been seduced by the same lie that he or she "who has the most toys in the end wins," to quote a well-known bumper sticker. It is noteworthy that both Jesus and Paul condemned the "love of money," a love that seems to have consumed far too many in our day. "You cannot serve God and money," Jesus said.[19] And Paul bluntly, but rightly, stated that "the love of money is a root of all kinds of evil."[20] It is important to notice that Paul did not say that monetary wealth is *the* root of evil, but the *love* of wealth is *a* root, that is, one of the key sources of evil in this world.[21]

Moreover, during the past twenty years or so, a number of prominent American televangelists have arisen who have made the heart of their preaching what has been called "the health and wealth gospel," essentially teaching that Christians, as the children of God, should be rich and healthy. And if they are not, then they are living a sub-standard Christian life. The impact of this teaching has not been limited to North America but can be found in other parts of the world, even Africa. But, as the New Testament scholar Gordon Fee has argued, such teaching is a travesty of what the New Testament teaches about money and possessions.[22] These televangelists are simply promoting "materialism…and foolish carnality" with a Christian veneer.[23] And Augustine would say that Christians who have bought into Western materialism or the error of the "health and wealth" gospel are being rebuked by God in the current crisis. They need to go back to the teachings of the New Testament and completely re-evaluate their thinking about wealth.

LEARNING FROM THE APOSTLE PAUL ABOUT GENEROSITY

A significant amount of the New Testament deals with money matters,[24] an indication that how we use our money, the choices we make in spending and investing, is a vital area of person's life in this world. In the final analysis, our use of money says much about what we consider truly important in life. For example, one of the texts to which Augustine refers in his response to the losses caused by the fall of Rome is 1 Timothy 6:17-19, where Paul states:

> As for the rich in this present age, charge them not to be haughty, nor to set their hopes on the uncertainty of riches, but on God, who richly provides us with everything to enjoy. They are to do good, to be rich in good works, to be generous and ready to share, thus storing up treasure for themselves as a good foundation for the future, so that they may take hold of that which is truly life.[25]

In a world in which God is the One who ultimately controls the future and the destinies of nations and even individuals, Paul does not doubt for a moment that the possession of wealth is a gift from an all-generous God. Those who have been so blessed, though, have the responsibility to show themselves good stewards of God's bounty. They are not to think that their wealth makes them a cut above other men and women. Nor are they to put their trust in their money and possessions.[26] Such things, as we have definitely seen in the current financial crisis, can disappear overnight. Rather, they are to trust in the Giver, not his gifts. They are to be generous towards those in need, a keynote of Paul's ministry, as we shall explore further. Such faithfulness in the use of riches earns rich spiritual dividends, both in this age and in the life to come.[27]

It used to be common to think that the early Christian movement consisted almost totally of poor people and slaves.[28] Bible scholars are increasingly convinced, though, that the actual social and economic status of the early Christians was far more complex. There were wealthy believers in the churches founded by Paul, men like Erastus, the city treasurer of Corinth, and Aquila and Priscilla, who were well-off enough to set up leatherworking shops in a number of cities, including Rome, Corinth and Ephesus.[29] Furthermore, those who provided their homes as meeting-places for those converted through Paul's mission, like Lydia in Philippi and Philemon in Colossae,[30] also had to be well-off since this would have required a spacious area that simply did not exist in the homes of the poor.[31] These rich Christians knew what it meant to use their wealth "to do good" and "to be generous" (1 Timothy 6:18).

It is evident from this advice in 1 Timothy 6 that Paul appreciated what money could do in helping people and expanding the Kingdom of Christ. For instance, one of the major aspects of Paul's life during the A.D. 50s was the supervision of a large collection of money for poor Christians in Jerusalem, where Christianity had had its origins. In the early days of its history, the first Christian community at Jerusalem had exuberantly sold their real estate and many of their personal possessions, "had all things in common," and sought to ensure that there were no poor among them.[32] In doing this, these men and women were not seeking to obey any explicit commandment from their Lord, Jesus Christ. Rather, they were simply motivated by a desire to make manifest and plain for all to see that in Christ they had "one heart and one soul" when it came to spiritual matters. The physical was a way of manifesting a profound spiritual reality.[33]

In disposing of their financial reserves in this way, however, the community placed itself in a highly vulnerable position when it came to finances. Persecution by Jewish leaders would have only aggravated their financial situation.[34] During the A.D. 40s, there was a series of food shortages in Palestine and then a particularly severe famine in A.D. 48 that appear to have triggered a financial crisis in the Jerusalem church.[35] Thus, when the Apostle Paul went up to Jerusalem in the very year that this famine struck, he was specifically asked by the leaders there to "remember the poor."[36]

In making this suggestion, the leaders of the Jerusalem church little knew how this project of collecting money to relieve the poverty of the Jerusalem Christians would become a major part of Paul's life and ministry for nearly a decade. The Collection, for so it has come to be called, involved the making of elaborate plans to gather together what was a substantial amount of money from the various churches that Paul had established among the Greeks and Romans. Many in these churches were not wealthy but they were determined to help those suffering in the midst of financial hardship in Palestine.[37] And once this generous gift of money was gathered, it was delivered to the Jewish Christians in Jerusalem. Paul came to see that this Collection was also a marvelous opportunity to demonstrate to the Jerusalem church and Jewish believers everywhere that even as they had one Lord and proclaimed one gospel, so also Jewish and non-Jewish Christians were together one people of God.[38] In both these ways, the Collection was a wonderful demonstration of the proper use of money that Paul recommends in 1 Timothy 6.

IMITATING THE MINDSET OF CHRISTIAN PHILANTHROPISTS

Of course, down through the years Christians and Christian philanthropists have used money in various other ways to benefit people and extend the Kingdom of Christ. For example, one of the most important Christian leaders of the third century was Cyprian, a North African Christian who was killed for his faith in A.D. 258. At the time of his conversion he was an extremely rich man. Realizing that he had far more than he needed to live on, he sold off his estates and gave the proceeds of the sale to the poor.[39]

Again, in the early eighteenth century, a number of major hospitals were founded by Christians who were "seriously rich."[40] One of them was Thomas Guy, a Baptist layman who was an enormously successful bookseller and printer of Bibles.

Not long before his death in 1724, he endowed what has become known as Guy's Hospital in London with a gift of £219,000—an astronomical amount in that day![41] Later in that century, Selina Hastings, the Countess of Huntingdon, used much of the significant wealth that became hers when her husband died to build churches where the Christian message could be proclaimed and people strengthened in their faith.[42] In the following century, Cyrus McCormick, who became very wealthy through his invention of the mechanical reaper that revolutionized the harvesting of grain, gave a $100,000 gift to his friend, the evangelist Dwight L. Moody, to begin what would later become Moody Bible Institute in Chicago.[43]

While comparative gifts of this kind are beyond the means of nearly all Western Christians today, there is little doubt that in the larger scheme of things, those in the West are rich compared with the rest of the world.[44] The current economic distress that we are feeling should not cause us to clam up and hoard our money. Rather, in this time when others are hurting, we need to "be generous and ready to share."[45]

TURNING TO PRAYER AS IN THE PANIC OF 1857

Of course, the recent crash on Wall Street is not the first time that Wall Street and other stock markets have taken such a radical plunge. One particularly instructive example occurred in 1857. Due to the gold rush in California, numerous banks in the 1850s began issuing far too many bank notes. What appeared on the surface to be a flood-tide of marvelous prosperity led to a boom in building railroads—"the railroad mania" in the words of one newspaper reporter[46]— and other building projects, a goodly number of which were being financed with extensive loans. Excessive importation of European goods, especially luxury items, led to further indebtedness. It was a credit bubble waiting to burst.

Suddenly, in August 1857, the Ohio Life Insurance and

Trust Company, which was essentially a bank of deposit and which was thought to be "the safest and soundest banking institution in all the West,"[47] had to suspend operations. It was based in Cincinnati but had a very important branch in New York City. When this branch failed, it soon brought down its Ohio headquarters, and shares in the company fell by 85% within four days. Since most of the other banks in New York were creditors of this New York branch, when it collapsed, there was panic on Wall Street. Although the New York banks were able to resume operations by that December, the long-term result of the Panic was devastating. In the words of historian Kenneth Stampp, there were "more than 5,000 business failures, as well as disastrous losses to countless investors in farmlands, town properties, railroad bonds and other securities."[48] In New York alone, some 20,000 New Yorkers lost their jobs.[49] Samuel Irenaeus Prime (1812-1885), the editor of the *New York Observer*, described the event at the time as "a sudden and fearful convulsion in the commercial world" in which "the sources of prosperity dried up, fortunes taking to themselves wings; houses, venerable for years, integrity and success, tumbling into ruins; and names, never tarnished by suspicion, becoming less than nothing in general bankruptcy."[50]

In the midst of this financial crisis, some New York Christians turned to prayer. One man in particular is remembered in this regard: Jeremiah Calvin Lanphier (1809-*c.*1898). Lanphier had come from a small town, seeking the opportunities a big city like New York afforded. After twenty years as a businessman in the city, he had become an evangelist. In September 1857, he invited "merchants, mechanics, clerks…and business men" to join him in praying to God "amid the perplexities" of the day.[51] At the first prayer meeting, at noon on Wednesday, September 23, 1857, in the North Reformed Dutch Church on Fulton Street, six people joined Lanphier. The following week there were twenty present. Prior to the third prayer meeting, on October 7, Lanphier specifically "prayed that the Lord would incline many to come to the place of prayer."[52] Forty came. Over the course of the next month, so many desired to pray that the noon-day meetings had to be held every day.[53] Within six months of the first prayer-meeting at the Dutch Church, there were crowded prayer-meetings taking place in twenty-one locations throughout Manhattan and similar meetings for prayer happening in numerous other American cities and towns, some of which had arisen around the same time as the one on Fulton Street.[54]

And as people genuinely sought God—albeit a good number because of the economic difficulties—God heard their prayers and a tremendous revival of biblical Christianity swept the United States between 1857 and 1859.[55] In the New York City area alone there were some 25,000 converts in the first three months of 1858.[56] Nationwide, the Methodists claimed to have received 180,000 new converts during the revival.[57] Churches were filled to capacity, and other venues, like public halls and theaters, had to be used for services.[58] "Everywhere religion seemed to be the common topic of conversation," an early twentieth-century Christian author, Frank Beardsley, noted.[59] Moreover, it is noteworthy that many of the revival preachers of this time, as historian Timothy Smith has observed, "issued repeated warnings against the danger that the love of money would benumb" concern for the poor. Relieving the impoverishment of the poor was a central feature of the churches of this era, and that partly because of the revival.[60]

In Chicago, Dwight L. Moody, a young Christian who would later become one of the most prominent evangelists of the late nineteenth century, noted in a letter to his mother, on January 6, 1857, that he had nothing to tell her that would interest her apart from news about "a great revival of religion in this city." Moody went on to tell his mother that he was going to church every night. "Oh, how I do enjoy it! It seems

JEREMIAH LANPHIER (1809-*c*.1898)

as if God was here Himself."[61] The fact that this letter was written in January 1857, that is, before the Panic of 1857, indicates that the origin of the revival cannot be solely tied to the financial woes that have been described above.[62] Before the bear market that descended upon America in the fall of 1857, God was already at work. In Missouri, during the course of 1858, churches in fifty towns reported 2,000 converts, and the preaching of J. B. Fuller, a converted English actor and the nephew of a famous theologian, Andrew Fuller, had an enormous impact.[63] All in all, this awakening of 1857–1859 saw up to a million converts in America and would be hailed by contemporaries as the "event of the century."[64]

The revival was not restricted to North America. In 1858 it leaped across the Atlantic to the British Isles—a common language, a common culture and a common Evangelicalism facilitating such a crossing. A financial crisis of proportions similar to that which had gripped America had descended upon Britain.[65] It is estimated that a million people or so in Great Britain also became Christians during this time of spiritual awakening.[66]

TRUSTING GOD LIKE J. C. PENNEY

One of the most respected chains of American department stores is the J.C. Penney Company. Its origins can be traced to a store started in 1902 by James Cash Penney, the son of a Kentucky Baptist minister, in Kemmerer, Wyoming.[67] It was incorporated under its present name in 1913 and by 1929 Penney himself was worth forty million dollars. But 1929 was the year of the stock market crash. The store's stock plunged from 120 points to 13, and Penney himself lost almost his entire fortune. Crushed by this sudden reversal and plagued by unrelenting financial worries, Penney's health began to suffer. "I was so harassed with worries that I couldn't sleep and developed an extremely painful ailment," he later admitted. In 1931 he decided to admit himself into the Kellogg Sanitarium in Battle Creek, Michigan, where one of the resident doctors told him that he was extremely ill.

"A rigid treatment was prescribed, but nothing helped," Penney recalled in his memoirs. But the problem was deeper than physical. Penney felt that he had no one to turn to for help and comfort and was rapidly losing any will to live. "I got weaker day by day. I was broken nervously and physically, filled with despair, unable to see even a ray of hope. I had nothing to live for. I felt I hadn't a friend left in the world, that even my family had turned against me."

One particular night Penney awoke with the strange con-

J.C. PENNEY (1902-1971)

viction that he would die that very night. "Getting out of bed, I wrote farewell letters to my wife and son, saying that I did not expect to live to see the dawn." But Penney was wrong. He awoke the following morning, still very much alive. As he was walking down a hallway in the hospital later that morning, he heard singing coming from a little chapel on the premises of the sanatorium. A hymn, "God will take care of you," written by Civilla D. Martin in 1904, was being sung. Penney entered the chapel, sat down, and was transformed as he listened to the following lines of the hymn:

> *Be not dismayed whate'er betide,*
> *God will take care of you;*
> *Beneath His wings of love abide,*
> *God will take care of you.*

> *God will take care of you,*
> *Through ev'ry day, o'er all the way;*
> *He will take care of you,*
> *God will take care of you.*

Then someone read from Matthew 11:28-30: "Come unto me, all you that are heavy laden, and I will give you rest. Take my yoke upon you, and learn of me; for I am meek and lowly in heart, and you shall find rest for your souls. For my yoke is easy and my burden is light." Penney found himself praying to God, "Lord, I can do nothing. Will you take care of me?" "Suddenly something happened," he said later. "I had a feeling of being lifted out of an immensity of dark space into a spaciousness of warm and brilliant sunlight...God with his boundless love and matchlessly patient love was there to help me. God had answered me when I cried out, 'Lord, I can do nothing. Will you take care of me?'" Penney realized that he had not followed Christ's teaching as his parents had taught him and he had not loved God as he ought to have. Passages like Matthew 16:26 began to powerfully transform his way of thinking: "What profit is it to a man if he gains the whole world, and loses his own soul? Or what will a man give in exchange for his soul?" He came to realize that above all he needed to "learn the anatomy of humility," the humility that marked the life of Christ his Savior.

Having the strength to rebuild his life and business, Penney started afresh in 1932 with money borrowed from his life insurance, and by the early 1950s the company sales surpassed a billion dollars. In the words of Mary Curry, Penney became "one of America's greatest merchants and is a continuing role model for achieving business success."[68] What is critical in the life of Penney is not so much the success of the company subsequent to his conversion to Christianity, but the ability he was given to rebuild his life on trust in God.

"IN GOD WE TRUST"

How then should we respond to this financial crisis? This booklet has argued that instead of panic and despair, Christians need to exercise that trust commended on American coinage, "In God we trust." God is sovereign over all of the affairs of men—the good times and the bad—and is working out his purposes in history to bring glory to Jesus Christ. Whatever losses we experience during the bad financial times upon us, we cannot lose God and the spiritual wealth that comes from being a Christian.

In such times as these, it would be so easy and so natural to keep to ourselves what financial resources we have left. While provision needs to be made for our own families,[69] times like these call for open hands and generosity on the part of those who call Christ, Lord. The words of Augustine's mentor, the Apostle Paul, are as germane as ever: "as we have opportunity, let us do good to everyone."

Finally, who knows how God will use these major financial woes and setbacks. In the past, crises such as the Panic of 1857 and the Depression of the 1930s became a means to convince many—for example, men like J.C. Penney—who had trusted in uncertain riches, of the folly of such trust and to put their faith in Christ instead. Oh, may this current economic crisis cause many to call out to God in sincerity and find Christ. All who do so can face the uncertainties of the future with confidence and say, "The Lord is my helper; I will not fear."[70]

ENDNOTES

1   For help in writing this pamphlet, I am indebted to David Clark of Welwyn, England, and my research assistant, Rev. Steve Weaver.

2   Michael Lewis, ed., *Panic: The Story of Modern Financial Insanity* (New York: W.W. Norton & Co., 2008).

3   Paul Krugman, *The Return of Depression Economics and the Crisis of 2008* (New York: W.W. Norton & Co., 2009).

4   David R. Wilkerson, *America's Last Call* (Lindale, TX: Wilkerson Trust Publications, 1998), 21-30. The term "financial holocaust" appeared on the cover.

5   Anastasia Nesvetailova and Ronen Palan, "A Very North Atlantic Credit Crunch: Geopolitical Implications of the Global Liquidity Crisis," *Journal of International Affairs*, 62, No.1 (Fall/Winter 2008), 165-185.

6   See Revelation 18.

7   See, for example, Acts 1:6-7, where Jesus clearly tells the Apostles that there are limits to their knowledge of God's sovereign workings in history.

8   C.S. Lewis, *The Problem of Pain* (New York: HarperCollins, 1996), 91.

9   Niall Ferguson, *The Ascent of Money: A Financial History of the World* (New York: Penguin Press, 2008), 163.

10 Here I assume a Christian perspective on the linear nature of history. The realm of history is not cyclical, as the ancient Greeks argued, but is proceeding along a line, as it were, with a beginning in the past and an end in the future.

11 As I was writing this, I came across the following online headline regarding the presidency of Barack Obama: "Challenges ahead, but Obama can learn from the past" (CTV.ca, January 18, 2009).

12 Augustine, *City of God* 1.7. Translated by Henry Bettenson, *St. Augustine: Concerning the City of God against the Pagans* (New York: Penguin Books, 2003), 12.

13 Augustine, *City of God* 1.14-16.

14 Augustine, *City of God* 1.10.

15 1 Timothy 6:6.

16 1 Timothy 6:8.

17 Job 1:21.

18 Augustine is quoting from 1 Timothy 6:9.

19 Matthew 6:24. See also Luke 16:13.

20 1 Timothy 6:10.

21 Elsewhere in the Bible, the Pharisees, often found as opponents of Jesus, are described as "lovers of money" (Luke 16:14). Paul states that a bishop/overseer should not be a "lover of money" (1 Timothy 3:3; see also Titus 1:7). And the anonymous writer of Hebrews urges his readers to keep themselves free from the love of money (Hebrews 13:5).

22 Gordon Fee, *The Disease of the Health and Wealth Gospels* (Vancouver: Regent College Publishing, 1985).

23 Bobby Ross Jr., "Prosperity Gospel on Skid Row," *Christianity Today*, 53, No.2 (February 2009), 12.

24 See, for example, Matthew 6:19-21,24-34; 13:12,44-46; Mark 10:17-31; Luke 12:13-34; 16:1-13; 18:18-30.

25 Augustine quotes this text in *City of God* 1.10.

26 The folly of putting one's trust in riches is a common theme in the Bible. See Psalm 62:10; Proverbs 23:4-5; Jeremiah 9:23; 1 Timothy 6:10.

27 D.B. Knox, "Wealth." In J.D. Douglas and N. Hillyer, eds. *The Illustrated Bible Dictionary* (Leicester: Inter-Varsity Press, 1980), 3:1633.

28 This was based on a reading of 1 Corinthians 1:26, where Paul says that among the Corinthians there were not "many...of noble birth."

29 For Erastus, see Romans 16:23; for Aquila and Priscilla, see Acts 18:1-3; Romans 16:3-5; 1 Corinthians 16:19; 2 Timothy 4:19. For differing views on their social status, see Florence Morgan Gillman, "Erastus." In David Noel Freedman, ed. *The Anchor Bible Dictionary* (New York: Doubleday, 1992), 2:571. And, Peter Lampe, "Aquila." In *The Anchor Bible Dictionary*, 1:319-320.

30 Acts 16:11-15; Philemon 1-2.

31 In addition to Aquila, Priscilla, Lydia and Philemon, see also Romans 16:1-2 (Phoebe, who was probably the owner of the house in which the church at Cenchreae met); Romans 16:23 (Gaius who was "host...to the whole church" in Corinth); and Colossians 4:15 ("Nympha and the church in her house" in Colossae).

32 Acts 2:44-45; 4:32-35.

33 Acts 4:32; Max Scheler, *Ressentiment*, L.A. Coser, ed. Translated by W.W. Holdheim (New York: Schocken Books, 1972), 111-112.

34 Compare the persecution described in Hebrews 10:33-34, where the loss of material possessions and goods was involved.

35 Keith F. Nickle, *The Collection: A Study in Paul's Strategy* (Naperville, IL: Allenson, 1966), 24, 29-32; S. McKnight, "Collection for the Saints." In Gerald F. Hawthorne, Ralph P. Martin, Daniel G. Reid, eds. *Dictionary of Paul and His Letters* (Downers Grove, IL: InterVarsity Press, 1993), 144.

36 Galatians 2:10.

37 See 1 Corinthians 16:1-4; 2 Corinthians 8-9. The reference in 2 Corinthians 8:20 to this collection being a "lavish gift" points to the substantial amount of money involved.

38 Romans 15:25-28. See also McKnight, "Collection for the Saints", 145.

39 Pontius, *The Life of Cyprian*, 2.

40 Matthew Bishop and Michael Green, *Philanthrocapitalism: How the Rich Can Save the World* (New York: Bloomsbury Press, 2008), 24.

41 For Guy's story, see Sydney Clark, "A generous miser," *Baptist Times* (February 24, 1994), 11.

42 See Faith Cook, *Selina, Countess of Huntingdon* (Edinburgh: The Banner of Truth Trust, 2001).

43 Leslie R. Keylock, "Bringing in the Sheaves: Cyrus McCormick." In John Woodbridge, ed., *More Than Conquerors* (Chicago: Moody Press, 1992), 328-331.

44 To get a good idea of how wealthy most of us are compared to the world

population as a whole, visit the website "Global Rich List" (www.globalrichlist.com). My attention was drawn to this website by the blog of a good friend, Kirk Wellum (redeemingthetime.blogspot.com).

45 1 Timothy 6:18.

46 John Bach McMaster, *A History of the People of the United States, from the Revolution to the Civil War* (New York: D. Appleton and Co., 1913), VIII, 288.

47 McMaster, *History of the People of the United States*, VIII, 291.

48 Kenneth M. Stampp, *America in 1857: A Nation on the Brink* (New York: Oxford University Press, 1990), 224. For details, see 213-229,

49 Charles R. Geisst, *Wall Street: A History* (New York: Oxford University Press, 1997), 48.

50 Samuel I. Prime, *The Power of Prayer. Illustrated in the Wonderful Displays of Divine Grace at the Fulton Street and Other Meetings in New York and Elsewhere, in 1857 and 1858* (1859; reprint, Edinburgh: The Banner of Truth Trust, 1991), 1.

51 From "How Often Shall I Pray?", a handbill that Lanphier distributed in Lower Manhattan to advertise this prayer meeting. See J. Edwin Orr, *The Light of the Nations. Evangelical Renewal and Advance in the Nineteenth Century* (Grand Rapids: Wm. B. Eerdmans Publ. Co., 1965), 103. There is very little available on the life of Lanphier, but see Frank Grenville Beardsley, *A History of American Revivals* (3rd ed.; New York: American Tract Society, 1912), 218-219; Orr, *Light of the Nations*, 102-103; Margaret Bendroth, "'What Wilt Thou Have Me To Do?' Jeremiah Lanphier and Revival" in J. Woodbridge, ed. *More Than Conquerors*, 336-339; Norris A. Magnuson, "Lanphier, Jeremiah C(alvin)" in Donald M. Lewis, ed. *The Blackwell Dictionary of Evangelical Biography 1730-1860* (Oxford: Blackwell, 1995), II:670; Kathryn Teresa Long, *The Revival of 1857-58: Interpreting an American Religious Awakening* (New York: Oxford University Press, 1998), 13. A small biography of Jeremiah Lanphier is needed.

52 Prime, *Power of Prayer*, 8-9. Prime is quoting from Lanphier's diary.

53 Prime, *Power of Prayer*, 10.

54 John D. Hannah, "The Layman's Prayer Revival of 1858," *Bibliotheca Sacra* 134 (1977), 64-65; Timothy L. Smith, *Revivalism and Social Reform in Mid-Nineteenth-Century America* (New York: Abingdon Press, 1957), 66.

55 For details of this revival, known to historians as the Businessmen's Revival, see Orr, *Light of the Nations*, 101-125; Smith, *Revivalism and Social Reform*, 63-79; Roy J. Fish, *When Heaven Touched Earth. The Awakening of 1858 and Its Effects on Baptists*, Mack Tomlinson, ed. (Texas: Need of the Times Publishers, 1996).

56 Fish, *When Heaven Touched Earth*, 45.

57 Stampp, *America in 1857*, 238.

58 Stampp, *America in 1857*, 237.

59 Beardsley, *History of American Revivals*, 223.

60 Smith, *Revivalism and Social Reform*, 174.

61 Cited William R. Moody, *The Life of Dwight L. Moody* (New York: Fleming H. Revell Co., 1900), 47-48. In the words of Stanley N. Gundry, "Moody's roots [as an evangelist] were in the prayer revival of 1857-8" ["Demythologizing

Moody." In Timothy George, ed. *Mr Moody and the Evangelical Tradition* (London: T&T Clark, 2004), 19]. For a good study of Moody's life, see Lyle W. Dorsett, *A Passion for Souls. The Life of D.L. Moody* (Chicago: Moody Press, 1997). For the impact of the revival upon Chicago, see Orr, *Light of the Nations*, 123-125.

62 Beardsley, *History of American Revivals*, 217; Stampp, *America in 1857*, 237; Smith, *Revivalism and Social Reform*, 64.

63 Orr, *Light of the Nations*, 122.

64 Long, *Revival of 1857-58*, 3. Hannah, "Layman's Prayer Revival," 59, notes that the estimated number of converts ranges between 300,000 and one million. For this range, he is relying on Beardsley, *History of American Revivals*, 236-237. Beardsley himself "placed the number of converts at five hundred thousand" (*History of American Revivals*, 237). On the other hand, Warren A. Candler, *Great Revivals and the Great Republic* (Nashville: Publishing House of the Methodist Episcopal Church, South, 1904), 215-216, suggests that there were a million converts, which is the usual figure cited by secondary sources. For the latter, see J. Edwin Orr, *America's Great Revival* (Elizabethtown, PA: McBeth Press, 1957), 28-29.

65 See D. Morier Evans, *The History of the Commercial Crisis of 1857-1858 and the Stock Exchange Panic of 1859* (1859; reprint, Newton Abbot: David & Charles, 1969).

66 For overall details, see Orr, *Light of the Nations*, 126-155. On the revival as it impacted Wales, see Eifion Evans, *Two Welsh Revivalists: Humphrey Jones, Dafydd Morgan and the 1859 Revival in Wales* (Bridgend: Evangelical Library of Wales, 1985), and for the impact on Northern Ireland, see William Gibson, *The Year of Grace: A History of the Ulster Revival of 1859* (Reprint, Harrisonburg, VA: Sprinkle Publications, 1994).

67 For the following details about Penney, I am especially indebted to J.C. Penney, *Fifty Years with the Golden Rule* (New York: Harper & Brothers, 1950) and Robert Flood, "Living by the Golden Rule: J.C. Penney." In Woodbridge, ed. *More Than Conquerors*, 340-343. But I have also used Norman Beasley, *Main Street Merchant: The Story of the J.C. Penney Company* (New York/Toronto: Whittlesey House, 1948); Mary Elizabeth Curry, "Penney, J.C." In *American National Biography*, John A. Garraty and Mark C. Carnes eds. (New York: Oxford University Press, 1999), 17:297-299; Victor M. Parachin, "The Hymn That Saved J.C. Penney" (www.lifeway.com/lwc/article_main_page/0,1703,A%253D161090%2526M%25 3D50022,00.html; accessed January 24, 2009). His middle name *was* actually Cash, though there were some who thought he added it later as his business began to prosper!

68 Mary Curry, "Penney, J.C." In *American National Biography*, 17:299.

69 1 Timothy 5:8.

70 Galatians 6:8.

71 Simoney Girard notes that in the wake of the recent financial turmoil, "Christians on Wall Street set up prayer meetings at Merrill Lynch, Goldman Sachs, JP Morgan Chase, Citigroup and other troubled banks" ["Grace in hard times," *Evangelical Times*, 43, No.2 (February 2009), 20].

72 Hebrews 13:6.

MICHAEL A. G. HAYKIN

Born in England of Irish and Kurdish parents, Michael Haykin is currently Professor of Church History and Biblical Spirituality at The Southern Baptist Theological Seminary, Louisville, Kentucky, and Research Professor at the Irish Baptist College, a constituent college of Queen's University, Belfast, Northern Ireland. Dr. Haykin has a Th.D. in Church History from Wycliffe College and the University of Toronto (1982). He blogs at *Historia ecclesiastica* on the website of The Andrew Fuller Center for Baptist Studies (www.andrewfullercenter.org), a center for the advanced study of Baptist history located on the campus of Southern Seminary.

Revival Titles from Audubon Press

The New York City Prayer Revival of 1858 and its Lessons, *by James W Alexander*

(219 page pb) This is the first time it has been reprinted since 1859. The author was a key leader during this unforgettable time of Revival. In these pages he recounts, through this compilation and presentation of his many useful little tracts, the powerful movement of the Holy Spirit that began in the summer and autumn of 1857 and resulted in hundreds of thousands of conversions, in just a few years. Samuel Prime said that these pithy tracts, "were very brief, ...eminently practical, ...clothed with gracefulness, ...marked by cogent reasoning, ...and they leave an impression on the most cultivated minds!" May God be pleased to use this book toward giving us another visitation of His Spirit very soon! ....**$19.99/$13.99**

The New York Pulpit during the Prayer Revival of 1858, *By James W Alexander, et al*
(395 page pb) Originally published in 1858, this memorial volume of key sermons preached during the great prayer revival of 1858 is a beautiful portrayal of God-owned Bible exposition. These twenty-five preachers, headed by James W Alexander, are a compilation of evangelistic preaching that we know was mightily used of God. Urgent themes like the coming Day of Judgment, unregenerate man's need for evangelical repentance, and passionate pleadings for unconverted man to seek the Lord while He may be found, characterize this book. This is the type of preaching that God uses in revival! ....**$27.99/$19.59**

To Order Your Copy of these informative Titles, Contact Audubon Press Today!

Living for Jesus, *By Robert L Dickie*
(302 page pb, $14.95)

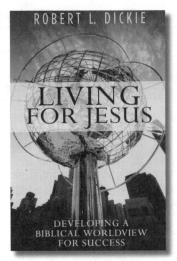

In these difficult times, what is a Biblical worldview? Where can we find a map that shows us how to live the spiritual journey of life? Without such a map, people tend to wander and stumble along without any real sense of purpose.

Starting with the creation mandate, Pastor Bob Dickie leads us, in a practical and relevant way, to a clear understanding of what it means to live every day for Jesus.

"Outstanding for its relevance in our 21st-century environment..."
Erroll Hulse

"Read it, study it and apply it..."
Vernon Higham

"Don't just read this book once. Read this over and over until the lessons of *Living for Jesus* are in the core of who you are."
Orrin Woodward

EMMAUS ROAD PRESS

Audubon Press
& Christian Book Service